FRANCIS FRITH'S
A TASTE OF THE NORTH-EAST

Dearest Phyll,

Happy Birthday Dear.

I hope that you enjoy your walk down memory lane .

All my Love

Michael xxx

THE FRANCIS FRITH COLLECTION

www.francisfrith.com

FRANCIS FRITH'S

A Taste of
THE NORTH-EAST

REGIONAL RECIPES FROM NORTHUMBERLAND,
TYNE & WEAR AND COUNTY DURHAM

Illustrated with historical photographs from
The Francis Frith Collection

FRANCIS FRITH'S

A Taste of
THE NORTH-EAST

Darlington, North Lodge Park 1911 63547

Compiled by Julia Skinner

First published in the United Kingdom by
The Francis Frith Collection exclusively for Identity Books in 2009
Paperback Edition ISBN 978-1-84589-452-8

British Library Cataloguing in Publication Data

A Taste of The North-East
Julia Skinner

The Francis Frith Collection®
Frith's Barn, Teffont,
Salisbury, Wiltshire SP3 5QP
Tel: +44 (0) 1722 716 376
Email: info@francisfrith.co.uk
www.francisfrith.com

Printed and bound in England

Front Cover: Durham, The Cathedral from the River 1921 70712t

The colour-tinting in this image is for illustrative purposes only, and is not intended
to be historically accurate.

CONTENTS

INTRODUCTION

Travel around the north-east of England through the pages of this book and discover a selection of the delicious traditional food of the area, as well as some of the stories and fascinating facts behind the recipes. Your journey will be given added savour by the delightful historical images taken by photographers from The Francis Frith Collection, showing the people and places of Northumberland, Tyne & Wear and County Durham in the past.

Regional traditional dishes were developed from the local produce that was available to thrifty housewives who needed to feed large, hungry families on a limited budget. Many old recipes also reflect the limited cookery techniques that were available in the past, as well as the skills of the cooks who were able to provide cheap and tasty meals with only a fire, a skillet and a cauldron to cook with, often producing the historical version of 'boil in the bag' meals.

This book is not intended to provide a comprehensive collection of the local recipes of the region, and some recipes are modern interpretations using some of the fine local produce that the area is famous for, but we hope that the food described within these pages, as well as the descriptions of local customs and dialect words, will provide you with a taste of the north-east of England.

Newcastle upon Tyne, The Quayside
1928 N16316

SOUPS AND SNACKS

RECIPE

_—·—_

Leek and Potato Soup

Leeks are a popular vegetable in the north-east of England, and in the past many areas held contests in the winter to find the local leek-growing champion.

  50g/2oz butter
  2 leeks, trimmed, washed and chopped
  1 small onion, finely chopped
  350g/12oz potatoes
  900ml/1½ pints chicken or vegetable stock
  Salt and pepper

Heat 25g/1oz of the butter in a large saucepan, add the leeks and onions and cook gently for 8-10 minutes, stirring occasionally to prevent sticking, until the vegetables are softened but not browned. Add the potatoes to the pan and cook, stirring occasionally, for a further 3-5 minutes, then add the stock and bring to the boil. Cover the pan and reduce the heat, then simmer gently for 30-40 minutes until the vegetables are very tender.

Season to taste. Remove the pan from the heat and stir in the remaining butter, then serve the soup whilst it is still piping hot, with good crusty bread.

This can be sieved or liquidised if a smoother soup is preferred, then serve with a swirl of cream and some freshly chopped parsley to finish.

_—·—_

West Hartlepool, A Tram in Church Street 1901   46944x

RECIPE

— . —

Pease Pudding

'Pease Pudding Hot!'
Pease Pudding has been a popular snack in the north-east for hundreds
of years, and was commonly sold by street vendors in the 19th century.
It can be eaten by itself, or as an accompaniment to roast pork, ham or
bacon, or slices can be fried in bacon dripping to serve for breakfast.

> 225g/8oz yellow split peas
> 1 onion, finely chopped
> 25g/1oz butter
> 1 beaten egg
> Stock – bacon stock is best

Soak the peas overnight, then drain. Put the peas and chopped onion
in a pan, with enough stock to cover them. Bring to the boil, then cover
the pan with the lid, reduce the heat and simmer until the peas are quite
soft, adding more stock if necessary. Allow to cool slightly, then sieve or
liquidise. Beat in the butter and egg, and test for seasoning.

Pour the mixture into a greased pie dish, cover with a lid or foil and cook
for half an hour in a pre-heated oven at 160°C/325°F/Gas Mark 3.

— . —

Sunderland, Shipyards on the Wear c1900 S263508

650 years of shipbuilding on the Wear came to an end with the closure of North East Shipbuilder's Southwick yard in 1989. Here, however, is a reminder of what it used to be like, with ships being fitted out on both sides of the river.

Carling Peas

Carling peas are said to have once rescued the people of Newcastle from starvation, although there are differing versions of the tale. One version is set during the Civil War, when Royalist Newcastle was besieged from July to October in 1644 by the Scots, who wanted to capture the town and control the coal supplies for the Parliamentarian cause. Food supplies in the town ran out and the people were starving, but in the nick of time a foreign ship managed to evade the blockade and reach port with its cargo of carling peas. Another tradition dates the event even earlier, to 1327, when Scottish forces under Robert the Bruce besieged Newcastle. However, both traditions agree that the life-saving peas were distributed to the starving people of Newcastle on Passion Sunday, which was why Carlins were eaten on that day in commemoration of the event.

Newcastle upon Tyne, Grainger Street 1900 N16314

RECIPE

—·—

Carlins

In former times, split and dried peas were eaten much more commonly than nowadays, and were a good source of protein. As well as pease pudding, another popular north-eastern dish made with peas is Carlins. This dish used to be served on the fifth Sunday after Lent, known as Passion – or Carling – Sunday, and for this reason Passion Sunday was often also known as 'Pea Sunday'. The name 'Carling' derives from an old name for 'mourning', in memory of Christ's Passion.

There are several versions of recipes for Carlins, but the Northumberland version is given here. The traditional peas to use should be Carling peas, also known as maple peas, black peas or pigeon peas, but dried green peas can also be used.

> 225g/8oz carling peas, or dried green peas
> 50g/2oz butter (traditionally this would be lard)
> Salt and pepper
> Vinegar

Soak the peas overnight in plenty of water, then strain. Put the peas in a saucepan, cover with fresh water and bring to the boil. Simmer for 20-30 minutes, until the peas are soft, then strain. Melt the butter in a saucepan, add the peas and fry them for a few minutes, shaking the pan occasionally to make sure the peas do not burn. Serve the peas hot, seasoned with plenty of salt, pepper and a dash of vinegar, to taste.

—·—

A Taste of the NORTH-EAST

Durham, Elvet Bridge 1918 68236

RECIPE

— · —

Bacon Floddies

Bacon Floddies are a traditional dish from Gateshead and Durham. They can be served on their own, but are usually served with sausages or bacon and eggs for breakfast or supper.

225g/8oz peeled potatoes

2 medium onions, peeled

175g/6oz bacon rashers, finely chopped

50g/2oz self-raising flour

Salt and freshly ground black pepper

2 eggs, beaten

4 tablespoonfuls bacon dripping or oil

Grate the potatoes and onion into a mixing bowl. Add the finely chopped bacon, the flour and the seasoning and mix well. Add the beaten eggs, mixing them well through all the ingredients. Heat the dripping or oil in a heavy pan until hot but not smoking. Add tablespoons of the floddies to the pan, not overcrowding them, and fry carefully on both sides until they are golden and cooked through. Drain on paper towels and keep hot in a dish until ready to serve.

— · —

Hadrian's Wall

Hadrian's Wall was built out of stone and turf by the Romans in the 2nd century AD, stretching for 73 miles across Britain from Bowness on the west coast to Wallsend on the east. It spanned the entire width of Britain and was the northern border of the Roman province of Britannia for hundreds of years.

The Roman fort of Vindolandia stands between Bardon Mill and Once Brewed. In 1973 fragments of 1,500 wooden tablets were discovered at Vindolandia which were found to be an assortment of letters, administrative records and other trivia which provide fascinating detail about the everyday lives of the men - and women - stationed on the Wall, which must have seemed like a posting to the end of the known world. One of the fragments is a birthday party invitation from Claudia Severa, the wife of Brocchus (commander of an unidentified fort called Briga), to Sulpicia Lepidina, who lived at Vindolandia. Lepidina was the wife of Flavius Cerialis, the praefectus in command of Cohors IX Batavorum which occupied Vindolandia from around AD97 onwards.

> *'Claudia Severa to her Lepidina, greetings. On the third day before the Ides of September, sister, for the celebration of my birthday, I give you a warm invitation to make sure that you come to us, to make the day more enjoyable for me by your arrival, if you are present. Give my greetings to your Cerialis. My Aelius and my little son send him their greetings ...'*

What sort of food would Claudia have served to her guests at her birthday party? We know that a typical Roman dinner party could have included oysters, mussels and snails, boiled ham, roast venison, suckling pig, peacock and stuffed dormouse, and many of these foods would have been available to her in Northumberland.

Housesteads, Hadrian's Wall 1924 76657

FISH

Once, fishing was the livelihood of many people along the north-east coast. In the years immediately prior to the First World War, Northumberland fishing ports alone were landing in excess of 450,000 cwt of white fish a year: cod, haddock, whiting, ling, halibut, sole, dabfish, plaice, conger eel, coalfish and skate. On top of this were catches of mackerel, crabs, lobsters and periwinkles. The top ports for white fish were North Shields, Blyth and Newbiggin; for crabs it was Beadnell, Craster, Cullercoats, Holy Island and North Sunderland.

RECIPE

—.—

North Sea Fisherman's Pie

In former years a fish pie was the traditional dish to be eaten at Easter, on Good Friday.

For the filling:
350ml/12 fl oz milk
1 bay leaf
Half an onion, finely sliced
450g/1 lb haddock or cod fillet
225g/8oz smoked haddock fillet
3 hard-boiled eggs, chopped
25g/1oz butter or margarine
25g/1oz plain flour
75g/3oz shelled prawns
2 tablespoonfuls chopped fresh parsley
Lemon juice to taste

For the topping:
500g /1¼ lbs potatoes, cooked
40g/1½ oz butter
60ml/ 4 tablespoonfuls milk
115g/4oz grated hard cheese of choice
Salt and pepper

Place the milk, the bay leaf and sliced onion in a saucepan over a medium heat and add the fish. Cover, and poach the fish lightly for 10 minutes. Strain, discard the bay leaf and reserve the milk for the sauce. Flake the fish into a buttered pie dish, discarding the skin and any remaining bones. Add the chopped eggs to the fish.

Melt 25g/1oz butter in a saucepan on a low heat, stir in the flour and cook gently for 1 minute, stirring continually. Remove the pan from the heat and stir in the reserved milk that the fish was poached in, a little at a time and stirring continually so that no lumps are formed. When all the milk has been mixed in, return the pan to the heat and bring the mixture to the boil, stirring continually as the sauce thickens, then simmer the sauce for about 4 minutes, still stirring all the time. Remove from the heat and stir in the prawns.

Add the parsley, lemon juice and seasoning to taste. Pour the sauce over the fish and eggs in the pie dish, and gently mix it all together.

Pre-heat the oven to 180°C/350°F/Gas Mark 4.

To make the topping
Gently heat 40g/1½ oz butter in 60ml/ 4 tablespoonfuls of milk in a small saucepan until the butter melts, then add the milk and melted butter to the cooked potatoes, mash and then beat until smooth. Spoon over the fish pie mixture to cover, then score the surface with a fork. Sprinkle the grated cheese over the pie before baking.

Bake the pie in the pre-heated oven for 25-30 minutes, until the top is golden.

—.—

Seahouses, The Harbour c1965   S521093

Holy Island, A Pleasure Boat c1935 H348133

RECIPE

—— . ——

Mussels in Wine and Cream Sauce

Mussels are in season from September until May and are a favourite delicacy from the Northumberland coast, especially around Lindisfarne (Holy Island).

> 1kg/2.2 lbs of fresh mussels
> 1 onion, finely chopped
> 2 cloves of garlic, finely chopped (optional)
> 150ml/5 fl oz dry white wine
> 50g/2oz butter
> 1 large handful of finely chopped parsley
> 4 tablespoonfuls of cream (single or double)
> Salt and freshly ground black pepper

Scrub and wash the mussels thoroughly under cold running water, discarding any which do not open when tapped. Remove the 'beard' (the black strip used for breathing) from each mussel with a sharp knife.

Melt the butter in a large, heavy-bottomed saucepan. Add the chopped onion and garlic (if used) and cook for a few minutes on a medium heat until the onion has softened. Pour the white wine into the saucepan and bring to the boil, stirring occasionally. Add the prepared mussels and cover the pan with a lid. Cook the mussels on a high heat for several minutes, gently shaking the bottom of the pan several times during cooking, until the mussel shells have opened – this should take about 15 minutes.

Remove the mussels one by one as they open. Take each mussel out of its shell and place them in a colander covered with a cloth and set over a bowl of lightly boiling water, to keep warm whilst the sauce is prepared. Discard any mussels that have failed to open.

Boil the remaining liquid in the pan until it reduces to half. Stir in the cream and parsley. Taste the sauce, as it may already be quite salty, and season to taste with salt and freshly ground black pepper. Put the mussels in large individual bowls and pour the sauce over them. Serve immediately, with plenty of fresh crusty bread.

—— . ——

Mead

Mead is produced on the Holy Island of Lindisfarne, off the Northumberland coast. Mead is a potent drink made from honey, and in the past it was believed that drinking mead would increase virility; for this reason, newly-wed couples were advised to drink mead for a whole month after their wedding to increase their chance of a happy marriage, and the word 'honeymoon' originates from this ancient custom.

Holy Island, The Lindisfarne Priory c1940 H348012

Kippers

Herrings were once caught locally at Craster, but they are now brought in from elsewhere to be turned into the oak-smoked kippers for which Craster is renowned, in a process that can take up to sixteen hours. The kipper factory here was established at the turn of the 19th century.

The traditional way of cooking kippers is to 'jug' them. Wash the fish in cold water, and trim off the heads and tails if desired. Place the kippers tail up in a tall jug and fill up the jug with enough boiling water to cover the fish. Leave the fish to stand in the water for about 8-10 minutes, then remove from the jug and serve each fish topped with a knob of butter.

Kippers also make a delicious savoury tea-time snack. Trim 2 kippers or 4 kipper fillets, place in a bowl or jug, cover with boiling water and leave to stand for 5 minutes. Remove the fish from the water and drain, then remove the skin and bone from each fish to leave the flesh. Spread the kipper flesh onto toast, sprinkle with grated cheese and place under a hot grill just long enough for the cheese to brown.

Craster, The Harbour 1951 C352001

RECIPE

— . —

Herrings in Oatmeal

Herrings were a particularly important catch for north-eastern fishermen in the 19th century. Herrings, known to fishermen as the 'silver darlings', are particularly nutritious and were sought after as a staple part of the diet in Victorian times. A mustard sauce is a favourite accompaniment to herrings in many parts of north-east England.

> 4 herrings
> 50g/2oz medium oatmeal
> Half a teaspoonful of salt
> 25-50g/1-2oz butter
> Juice of half a lemon
> Chopped fresh parsley

Clean and bone the herrings, and dry them. Mix the salt in with the oatmeal, and use this to coat the herrings on both sides, pressing the oatmeal well into the fish. Melt the butter in a frying pan and fry the herrings for about 3 minutes on each side, adding more butter as necessary. Place the cooked fish on a hot dish and keep warm.

Add a little more butter to the pan, and when it is melted and frothy add the lemon juice, pour over the fish and sprinkle with chopped parsley, or alternatively serve the fish with mustard sauce if preferred (see recipe on opposite page).

— . —

RECIPE

—·—

Mustard Sauce

The original creation of dry mustard powder is attributed to a Mrs Clements of Durham. In 1720 Mrs Clements discovered that the strength and taste of mustard could be greatly improved if the mustard seed was ground in a mill and processed in much the same way as flour was made from wheat. Her business producing Durham Mustard became very successful, and was based in Saddler Street in the city. This mustard sauce can be used with chicken, ham, pork, bacon and sausages, but in the north-east of England it is often served as an accompaniment for fish, especially grilled or fried herring and mackerel. Mustard sauce was also used as a traditional accompaniment to the boar's head which was often served at Christmas.

> 25g/1oz butter
> 25g/1oz plain flour
> 1 teaspoonful of vinegar
> 1 teaspoonful of caster sugar
> Salt and pepper
> 1-2 teaspoonfuls mustard powder (according to taste)
> 300ml/½ pint milk

Melt the butter in a double saucepan. Stir in the flour, and add the milk a little at a time, stirring continuously. Bring to the boil, then simmer until the sauce thickens, still stirring. Remove from heat. Blend together the mustard powder, sugar and vinegar to a smooth cream and stir into the sauce, mixing well. Season to taste. Heat through just before serving, but do not let the sauce boil.

—·—

Hartlepool, The Beach 1903 49993

RECICE

—·—

Stuffed Mackerel with Gooseberry Sauce

Gooseberries have long been a traditional accompaniment to mackerel in English cookery. Cold smoked mackerel fillets are also delicious eaten with brown bread and butter and a portion of gooseberry jam as a relish.

4 mackerel, gutted and de-scaled
1 tablespoonful chopped parsley
1 tablespoonful chopped thyme
Half a teaspoonful grated lemon rind
1 tablespoonful lemon juice
25g/1oz soft white breadcrumbs
Seasoned flour
225g/8oz gooseberries
Sugar to taste
A little butter or oil

Wash and dry the mackerel and clean them. Mix the parsley, thyme, lemon rind, lemon juice and soft breadcrumbs and stuff the mackerel with this mixture. Roll the fish lightly in seasoned flour. Melt a little butter or oil in a baking pan and, when it is very hot, put in the mackerel. Put into the oven and bake at 180°C/350° F/Gas Mark 4 for 25 minutes, carefully turning the fish over halfway through.

Meanwhile, for the gooseberry sauce, simmer the gooseberries in a very little water until they are soft. Rub them through a sieve and sweeten lightly, with the sugar, to taste.

Warm the gooseberry sauce through before serving with the mackerel.

—·—

Northumberland Rivers

The many rivers and their tributaries that flow through Northumberland give rise to some of the wildest and most spectacular scenery in Britain. The Tyne rises from the highest point of the Pennines not far from the source of the River Tees. Berwick-on-Tweed, the most northerly town in England, sits on the mouth of the River Tweed. Other rivers such as the Rede, the Till, the Aln and the Wansbeck snake their way through the landscape. The larger rivers are well used by fishermen angling for sea-trout and salmon. At the Tweedmouth Feast every July a local girl is crowned as the Salmon Queen in a celebration of the salmon fishing industry which has been important to the town for centuries. The origins of the festival date back to the 12th century and the festival of St Boisil, celebrating the salmon run down the River Tweed.

RECIPE

— · —

Salmon with Cucumber Sauce

Salmon or trout served with a cream and cucumber sauce is a traditional hot dish in many parts of the north-east. This recipe continues the tradition but is a cold dish suitable for hot summer days.

> 1.8kg/4 lbs salmon, gutted and scaled
> A small amount of melted butter, for brushing on to the salmon
> 3 parsley or thyme sprigs
> Half a lemon, cut into 2 further segments
> 1 large cucumber, peeled
> 25g/1oz butter
> 115ml/4 fl oz dry white wine
> 3 tablespoonfuls of finely chopped dill
> 4 tablespoonfuls of sour cream, or natural yogurt if preferred
> Salt and pepper

Pre-heat the oven to 220°C/425°F/Gas Mark 7.

Season the salmon and brush it inside and out with melted butter. Place the herbs and lemon in the cavity. Wrap the salmon in foil, folding the edges together securely, then bake in the pre-heated oven for 15 minutes. Remove the fish from the oven and leave in the foil for 1 hour, then remove the skin from the salmon.

Meanwhile, halve the cucumber lengthways, scoop out the seeds, and dice the flesh. Place the cucumber in a colander, toss lightly with salt, leave for about 30 minutes to drain, then rinse well and pat dry.

Heat the butter in a small saucepan, add the cucumber and cook for about 2 minutes, until translucent but not soft. Add the wine to the pan and boil briskly until the cucumber is dry. Stir the dill and sour cream or yogurt into the cucumber. Season to taste and serve immediately with salmon.

— · —

MEAT

Inland from the Northumberland coast, the Cheviot Hills stand as a rampart between Scotland and England. For centuries the Border Reivers raided the towns and villages for their cattle and sheep. Now the grassy tracks that once echoed to the shouts of bandits and sounds of livestock being driven to market by the drovers are used by walkers and the peaceful grasslands at the northern part of Northumberland National Park are dotted with grazing Cheviot sheep.

STILL AT THE FRONT!

ALBION LAMP COMPANY, BIRMINGHAM

THE "ALBIONETTE"

Otterburn, England from Carter Bar c1955 O84024

Cyclists and ramblers regularly use these trails that take them through the Harthorpe Valley to the Cheviot Hills. Many of the places in Northumberland have quaint names such as Skirl Naked, Pity Me and Blaw Wearie.

Wooler, Skirl Naked c1955 W396003

RECImpE

— . —

Northumberland Panfotheram

This was a traditional dish made in farmhouse kitchens when a sheep
was killed.

450g/1lb potatoes
2 onions
4 lamb chops, or – even better – mutton chops if you
    can get them
A little fat or oil for frying
25g/1oz plain flour
300ml/ ½ pint of good brown stock, preferably made
    from lamb or mutton bones
Salt and pepper

Pre-heat the oven to 180°C/350°F/Gas Mark 4.

Peel and slice the potatoes and onions, and place them in layers in a
heavy casserole dish, seasoning each layer with salt and pepper. Heat
the fat or oil in a frying pan and fry the chops lightly on both sides
to seal the meat, then place the chops in the casserole on top of the
potatoes and onions.

Stir the flour into the fat left in the frying pan, gradually add the stock,
stirring continuously, and bring to the boil. Pour the stock over the
meat and vegetables in the casserole, and cover the casserole dish
with the lid. Cook in the pre-heated oven for about 1 hour.

— . —

Barnard Castle

The castle dominates the town of Barnard Castle. In November 1569, during the Rising in the North, it was held by Sir George Bowes, a loyal servant of Queen Elizabeth I, against a force led by Charles Neville, Sixth Earl of Westmoreland, and Thomas Percy, Earl of Northumberland. Prior to surrendering, Sir George wrote that his command had been reduced to: *'a very hard dyett and great want of bread, drynck and water; which was our only drynck, save I mixed yt with some wyne. I fownde the people in the castle in continuall mutenyes, seaking to leape the walls and run to the rebells'.*

Barnard Castle, The Castle and the River Tees 1898 41432

RECIPE

— · —

Mutton and Potato Pie

This dish from Northumberland is also known as Tattie Pot.

6 middle neck lamb or mutton chops
3 lambs' kidneys
2 black puddings
225g/8oz onions, sliced
675g/1½ lbs potatoes, peeled and sliced
Salt and pepper
300ml/ ½ pint white stock
A small amount of oil, or melted dripping or lard.

Trim off any excess fat from the lamb chops. Skin the kidneys and remove the core, and slice. Slice the black puddings. Fry the chops and kidneys on both sides in their own fat in a frying pan for a few minutes. Place the chops in an ovenproof casserole, then cover them with a layer each of kidney, black pudding, onions and potatoes, seasoning each layer with salt and pepper. Continue with the layers until all the ingredients have been used, making sure to finish with a layer of potatoes, then pour over the stock.

Brush the top layer of potatoes with the oil, or melted dripping or lard. Cover the casserole with its lid or foil, and bake in a moderate oven at 180°C/350°F/Gas Mark 4 for 2 hours.

— · —

Darlington, Victoria Road 1903 50007

RECIPE

— · —

Savoury Lamb Pie

For the pie filling:
450g/1 lb of lean lamb, cut into small cubes
1 dessertspoonful of plain flour
Salt and pepper
1 medium sized onion, sliced
1 large cooking apple, peeled, cored and thinly sliced
150ml/ ¼ pint stock, preferably made from lamb bones

For the scone topping:
175g/6oz self-raising flour
¼ teaspoonful of salt
1 teaspoonful chopped mixed herbs
25g/1oz margarine
25g/1oz lard
125ml/3-4fl oz milk

Pre-heat the oven to 180°C/350°F/Gas Mark 4.

Add salt and pepper to the flour. Toss the cubes of meat in the seasoned flour to coat them on all sides. Place the meat in a shallow 2 pint casserole, and sprinkle on the remaining seasoned flour. Layer the sliced onions on top of the meat, then the sliced apple, and pour over the water or stock. Cover the casserole with the lid, and bake in the pre-heated oven for 1½ to 2 hours, until the lamb is tender (the time depends on the quality of the lamb used).

Increase the oven heat to 220°C/425°F/Gas Mark 7, ready to add the scone topping.

To make the scone topping: place the self-raising flour in a bowl, and add the salt and herbs. Rub in the fats, then add as much of the milk as is needed to mix it all to a soft dough. Roll out the dough to about ½ cm (¼ inch) thick, and cut into rounds about 6cm (2½ inches) in diameter.

Take the casserole out of the oven. Arrange the scone rounds on top of the pie filling, and return the casserole to the oven without its lid. Bake for a further 25-30 minutes, until the scone top is golden and crusty.

— · —

Alnwick, Bondgate and Market Place c1955 A223017

RECIPE

Alnwick Stew

This layered stew of bacon, potatoes and onions is very simple to make, and is very tasty. It can be made using either fresh meat or cooked leftover ham or bacon from a joint, and can also be made using bacon off-cuts bought cheaply from a butcher, to make an economical and filling meal. Salt should not need to be added to this dish, as the meat will contain enough salt already.

> 900g/2 lb ham or bacon, such as forelock, hock or collar
> 675g/1½ lb potatoes, peeled and sliced
> 2 onions, sliced
> 1 bay leaf
> English mustard powder
> Water or vegetable stock
> Black pepper

Cut the meat into chunky cubes. Place a layer of chopped onions in the base of a large casserole dish, add a layer of ham and then a layer of sliced potatoes, seasoning each layer with a little pepper and mustard powder. Continue layering and seasoning, and finish with a layer of potatoes. Place the bay leaf on top and pour in enough cold water or stock to reach to just below the top layer of potatoes.

Cover the dish with its lid and cook in a pre-heated oven for 1½ hours at 180°C/350°F/Gas Mark 4. Remove the lid for the last half an hour of cooking time to brown and crisp the potatoes.

Bishop Auckland, Newgate Street 1914 67136

Local words and phrases from County Durham

'Ahint' - behind.

'Badly liked' - disliked.

'Bairn' - small child. 'Grand-bairns' - grandchildren.

'Bank' - hill.

'Beck' or 'burn' - a stream.

'Butterloggy' or 'butterlowey' - a butterfly.

'Chancetimes' - occasionally.

'Chimla' - chimney.

'Dickiehedgie' - a hedge-sparrow.

'Ha' waxed folk' - children.

'Hand's turn' - a stroke of work.

'Mackem' - a person from Sunderland.

'Skelp' - smack.

'Throng' - very busy, as in 'It were throng in there!'

'Tidy Betty' - a bottomless fender across the fire grate.

'Whisht!' - Hush, be quiet!

'Wishful' - desirous, wanting something.

RECIPE

— · —

Durham Beef Casserole with Savoury Dumplings

For the casserole:

675g/1½ lb of beef stewing steak

2 onions, peeled and sliced

4 carrots, sliced

Salt and pepper

1 level tablespoonful of flour

A small amount of fat or oil for frying

600ml/1 pint good brown stock

For the savoury dumplings:

25g/1oz butter or margarine

175g/6oz self-raising flour, sifted to remove any lumps

1 teaspoonful of dry English mustard powder

1 teaspoonful each of dried or fresh sage, thyme and parsley

Salt and black pepper

To make the casserole: Cut the meat into cubes, and discard any fat. Mix the salt and pepper into the flour, and toss the meat in the seasoned flour to cover all sides. Melt the fat or oil in a frying pan and fry the meat in batches for a few minutes, turning the cubes of meat so that they are sealed on all sides. Remove the meat and put into a large casserole dish.

Fry the onions in the pan, adding a little more fat or oil if necessary, until soft. Add the onions to the casserole, with the sliced carrots. Pour on the stock, and season to taste with salt and pepper. Cover the casserole with a lid and cook in a moderate oven for 1½-2 hours at 160°C/325°F/Gas Mark 3, until the meat is tender. Just before the end of the cooking time, make the dumplings.

To make the dumplings: Rub the butter or margarine into the flour, then mix in the mustard powder, herbs and seasoning, and add enough water for it all to be mixed into a soft dough. Flour your hands, and shape the mixture into about 12 small balls.

When the casserole has cooked for 1½-2 hours, check the seasoning, and then add the dumplings to the stew. Replace the lid and continue cooking for a further 15-20 minutes, until the dumplings have swollen up nicely. Serve piping hot.

— · —

VEGETABLE, CHEESE AND SUPPER DISHES

Durham, The Traffic Policeman
1954 D71032x

RECIPE

Pan Haggerty

This is a traditional dish from Northumberland. The name is said
to derive from the French word 'Hachis', meaning to chop or slice,
referring to the sliced vegetables which are used, but another theory
is that it comes from the Viking word 'hagga', meaning to hack.

60ml/4 tablespoonfuls of oil, or 50g/2oz butter
or dripping

450g/1 lb firm potatoes, thinly sliced

1 large onion, thinly sliced

115g/4oz grated mature cheese

Salt and pepper

Heat the oil (or butter or dripping) in a large, heavy frying pan.
Remove the pan from the heat and arrange alternate layers of potato,
onion and cheese, starting with a layer of potatoes and seasoning
each layer. Return the pan to the heat, and cook for 30 minutes,
starting over a low heat and then increasing it so that the underside
of the mixture browns.

Switch on the grill, and when good and hot place the pan under the
grill for 5-10 minutes to brown the top of the mixture. Slide the Pan
Haggerty on to a warm plate and serve cut into wedges, although it is
traditional to serve this dish from the pan in which it is cooked.

RECIPE

—·—

Leek Pudding

225g/8oz self-raising flour
75g/3oz shredded suet
Water to mix – about 6 tablespoonfuls
Salt and pepper
675g/1½ lbs leeks
225g/8oz of any cold meat left over from another meal, such as
    bacon or cooked minced beef or lamb

Trim, wash and finely slice the leeks, and dry thoroughly. Chop the cold meat into small pieces if necessary. Mix the meat with the leeks.

Mix the suet into the flour and salt, and stir in enough water to make a light dough which is still firm enough to roll out. Roll out the dough on to a lightly floured board, to a rectangular shape about ½ cm (¼ inch) thick. Spread the meat and leek filling onto the dough, leaving an edge of about 1cm (½ inch), and season the filling well with salt and pepper. Dampen the edges of the dough with water, and roll it all up loosely, like a Swiss roll. Press the ends firmly together to seal them. Wrap the roll loosely in a large piece of greased foil, enclosing it completely, and sealing the ends well.

Scald a strong cotton cloth big enough to wrap the pudding in. Roll the pudding in the cloth and tie the ends securely with string. (It is useful to make a string handle across the top as well, which is helpful when removing the pudding from the water after cooking.)

Fill a large saucepan two-thirds full of water, and bring to the boil. Put the pudding in the pan, put on the saucepan lid and bring the water back to the boil. Boil for two hours, keeping the water at boiling point and being sure to replenish the pan with more boiling water from the kettle when necessary to prevent the pan boiling dry.

Serve the pudding with a good gravy, either by itself or as an accompaniment to meat such as boiled bacon.

—·—

Monster Cabbage

The world's largest-ever cabbage was grown by William 'Tar' Collingwood of Swalwell, County Durham, whose prized cabbage weighed in at 56kg (8 stone 11 lbs) in 1865. The monster cabbage stood 1.27 metres (4ft 2ins) high and measured 6.5 metres (7 yards 5ins) round. Mr Collingwood lived in a house next to the Buck Inn, now the Poacher, and worked at Ridley's steelworks. 'The Swalwell Cabbage' was so heavy that it had to be put into a handcart to be carried to the Buck Inn where it was shown, and was so big that Mr Collingwood had to take down the gateposts of his garden to allow the cabbage to be wheeled out.

Ashington, Village Shop, Milburn Road c1955 A224022x

RECIPE

— . —

Celery Cheese

1 head of celery
Salt and pepper
A little milk
75g/3oz hard cheese
1 egg
Breadcrumbs for topping
A little butter

Pre-heat the oven to 350°F/180°C/Gas Mark 4.

Wash and trim the celery, grate or chop it very finely and put it into a saucepan. Add just enough milk to cover the celery. Season with salt and pepper. Bring to the boil, then reduce the heat and simmer gently for about 10 minutes, until the celery is tender, then leave to cool for a few minutes.

Grate the cheese and beat the egg. Mix the cheese and egg into the celery, then turn the mixture into a greased ovenproof dish. Cover the top with breadcrumbs, and dot with small pieces of butter. Bake in the pre-heated oven for 15-20 minutes until golden brown.

— . —

South Shields, King Street c1898 S162005

RECIPE

— · —

Whitley Goose

This old dish from Whitley Bay is actually made of cheese and onions, and not from goose. It can be served as a supper dish, or as an accompaniment to meat, ham or bacon.

> 4 medium sized onions, peeled but left whole
> 115g/4oz hard cheese
> Salt and pepper
> 450ml/ ¾ pint single cream
> 3-4 tablespoonfuls of fresh breadcrumbs
> 25g/1oz butter

Place the whole onions in a saucepan and cover with water, adding a little salt. Bring to the boil, and continue to boil for 15-20 minutes until the onions are soft and tender. Drain well, and leave the onions to cool.

Pre-heat the oven to 200°C/400°F/Gas Mark 6.

Chop the cooked onions roughly, mix the onion pieces with half the grated cheese and season. Grease an ovenproof dish. Turn the onion mixture in to the dish, pour over the cream and mix lightly. Sprinkle half the remaining grated cheese on top, then the breadcrumbs, and finish with the rest of the cheese. Dot the surface with small pieces of butter. Bake for 20-30 minutes until the top is golden.

— · —

Whitley Bay, View of the Links c1951 W246003

Newcastle upon Tyne, The Quayside 1896 N16320

Local words and phrases from the Newcastle & Tyneside area

'Bairn' - child.

'Canny' - pleasant, kind, good.

'Clarts' - mud, **'Clartin'** - messing about.

'Deeky' - look at.

'Fernietickles' - freckles.

'Galluses' - men's braces.

'Hacky' - dirty.

'Hinny' - young woman.

'Ken' - know.

'Marra' - mate, friend.

'Plodge' - to wade in water.

'Sand dancers' - the slang term for people from South Shields, a term that derives partly from the fact that the town boasts an attractive beach, and partly from its Yemeni population, the largest outside Yemen itself.

PUDDINGS AND DESSERTS

Newcastle upon Tyne, The Quayside 1928 N16316

RECIPE

—·—

Newcastle Pudding with Lemon Sauce

A traditional Newcastle Pudding is made by lining a pudding basin with buttered slices of bread, filling the basin with a milk and egg mixture, and then steaming for about 1 hour. It is then served with a lemon sauce. This modern version of Newcastle Pudding is baked in the oven in the same way as a Bread and Butter Pudding, but still incorporates the tradition of the lemon sauce.

> 600ml/1 pint of milk
> Grated zest of 1 lemon
> 2 tablespoonfuls of lemon curd
> 4 eggs, beaten
> 75g/3oz caster sugar
> 6 slices of white bread
> Butter

Warm the milk in a small saucepan, stir in the lemon zest, then cover and leave to infuse for about 1 hour. When the milk has infused, beat the eggs and sugar well together in a small bowl, then pour the mixture into the milk and whisk well to mix it together.

Remove the crusts from the bread slices, thickly butter each slice, then spread the slices with the lemon curd. Cut each slice of bread in half diagonally.

Use some of the butter to thoroughly grease a large ovenproof dish. Pour a small amount of the milk and egg mixture into the bottom of the dish, then arrange half the slices of bread over the bottom of the dish, with the spread sides facing up. Place the remaining slices in the dish to make a second layer, but this time place them spread sides down.

Strain and pour the milk mixture into the dish and over the bread slices (the bread slices should be completely covered with the milk mixture). Leave the pudding for a further 1 hour, to allow the milk mixture to soak into the bread.

Pre-heat the oven to 180°C/350°F/Gas Mark 4.

When the milk mixture has soaked into the bread, bake the pudding in the pre-heated oven for 35-40 minutes, until the pudding has set and the top is golden brown. Serve with cream or custard, or with a quick lemon sauce if preferred, made by melting 115g/4oz of lemon marmalade in a saucepan, stirring in the juice and grated zest of 1 lemon and serving immediately.

—·—

RECIPE

—.—

Ginger Sponge Pudding

Newcastle became a leading port because of its position on the River Tyne. For many years fruit and spices such as lemons and ginger have been imported into the port and distributed throughout the north of England.

This sponge pudding also makes a delicious soft gingerbread when eaten cold.

175g/6oz self-raising flour
75g/3oz caster sugar
1 heaped teaspoonful ground ginger
50ml/2fl oz milk
75g/3oz margarine
1 good tablespoonful of golden syrup
1 teaspoonful bicarbonate of soda
A little extra golden syrup to finish

Pre-heat the oven to 160°C/325°F/Gas Mark 3.

Mix the flour, sugar and ginger together. Put the milk, margarine and syrup into a large saucepan, and bring to the boil. Sir well, until the margarine and syrup have melted. Remove the pan from the heat and stir in the bicarbonate of soda.

Add the flour, sugar and ginger to the milk and syrup mixture, and mix it all well together. Turn the mixture into a well-greased cake tin 20cm (8inch) square, and bake just above the centre of the pre-heated oven for 30 minutes. Just before serving, warm a little extra golden syrup in a saucepan and pour over the pudding. Serve hot, with custard or cream.

—.—

South Shields, Frederick Street c1906 S162002

RECIPE

— . —

Gooseberry and Elderflower Cream

In the 19th century competitions were held in many places in the north-east in the summertime, in an attempt to find the grower of the biggest gooseberry.

> 500g/1½ lbs gooseberries
> 30ml/2 tablespoonfuls elderflower cordial
> 300ml/10 fl oz double cream
> 115g/4oz icing sugar

Place the gooseberries in a heavy saucepan, cover and cook over a low heat, shaking the pan occasionally until they are tender. Tip the gooseberries into a bowl, crush them with a heavy wooden spoon or potato masher, then leave them to cool completely. (The gooseberries can be sieved or pureed if a finer consistency is preferred.) Beat the cream until soft peaks form, then fold in half the crushed gooseberries. Sweeten with icing sugar to taste, and fold in the elderflower cordial. Sweeten the remaining gooseberries with icing sugar to taste. Put a layer of the cream mixture in four dessert dishes or tall glasses, and then a layer of crushed gooseberries, then cover and chill for at least one hour before serving.

— . —

Bagpipes

The world's only bagpipe museum can be found at Morpeth. More than 100 different sets of bagpipes from all over the world can be seen, including the local Northumbrian pipes. These are blown by a bellows tucked under the piper's arm, unlike Scottish pipes, which are blown by mouth. The music of Northumbrian pipes has been brought to worldwide notice in recent years through the work of the renowned folk musician Kathryn Tickell.

Morpeth, Bridge Street c1965 M251069

RECIPE

—·—

Rhubarb and Orange Fool

Like gooseberries, for many years rhubarb has been a favourite crop grown in the allotments and cottage gardens of the north-east. It is always best to cook the rhubarb with a little less sugar than you think you will need, and then add more to taste if it is still too tart.

> 400g/14oz rhubarb stalks
>
> 75g/3oz caster sugar
>
> Juice and grated zest of 1 orange
>
> 300ml/10fl oz carton of whipping cream

Trim the ends of the rhubarb stalks, and cut the stalks into manageable chunks.

Put the rhubarb into a pan with the sugar, orange juice and grated orange zest. Cover and simmer gently for about 10-15 minutes, stirring regularly. The rhubarb should be cooked until it is soft, but not mushy.

Taste the rhubarb and add more sugar, if needed. Allow the rhubarb to cool completely.

When the rhubarb is cold, whip the cream until it forms soft peaks. Fold the rhubarb mixture into the cream very gently, so that the cream does not lose its volume. Divide the mixture into four individual glasses or bowls, and chill before serving.

—·—

RECITE

—.—

North Country Tart

225g/8oz shortcrust pastry

2 tablespoonfuls of raspberry jam

50g/2oz butter

25g/1oz caster sugar

1 large tablespoonful of golden syrup

115g/4oz desiccated coconut

1 egg, beaten

Pre-heat the oven to 190°C/375°F/Gas Mark 5.

Roll out the pastry on a lightly floured surface, and use it to line a greased 20cm (8 inch) pie tin. Spread the base of the tart with raspberry jam.

Put the butter, sugar and golden syrup into a saucepan over a low heat, and stir gently until it has all melted. Stir in the coconut and beaten egg, and mix it together well. Turn the mixture into the pie tin, and bake in the pre-heated oven for 25-30 minutes, until the filling has set and the pastry is golden and crisp.

—.—

Darlington, South Park Lake 1923 74333

TEATIME AND BAKING

RECIPE

—·—

Durham Pikelets

These pikelets are a cross between a pancake and a crumpet.

225g/8oz self-raising flour
1 teaspoonful bicarbonate of soda
1 teaspoonful cream of tartar
40g/1½ oz margarine or lard
40g/1½ oz sugar
300ml/ ½ pint (approx) buttermilk or low-fat milk
Half a teaspoonful salt

Sift the flour, bicarbonate of soda, cream of tartar and salt together into
a bowl, then rub in the margarine or lard until the mixture resembles
fine breadcrumbs, and mix in the sugar. Make a well in the centre of
the mixture and stir in the buttermilk or milk, beating lightly to give a
dropping consistency. Drop the mixture in spoonfuls onto a hot, well-
greased griddle or heavy frying pan, and cook the pikelets a few at a time
for about 4 minutes on each side until they are golden brown, greasing
the griddle or pan well between each batch and taking care not to let the
pikelets burn. Serve hot, spread with plenty of butter, and jam if liked.

—·—

Durham, Old Elvet 1914 67127

RECIPE

—·—

Felton Spiced Loaf

This quick and easy recipe makes delicious spicy tea bread that does not include yeast. It is served cut into slices, either plain or buttered.

115g/4oz butter
115g/4oz caster sugar
2 eggs, beaten
50g/2oz ground almonds
115g/4oz self-raising flour
Half a teaspoonful mixed spice
175g/6oz mixed sultanas and currants
50g/2oz shredded peel (optional)
A little milk

Pre-heat the oven to 190°C/375°F/Gas Mark 5.

Cream together the butter and sugar until the mixture is light and fluffy, then carefully beat in the eggs, a little at a time - add a little of the flour to prevent the eggs curdling, if necessary. Stir the ground almonds into the mixture. Sieve the flour and mixed spice together and stir into the mixture as well, together with the dried fruit and peel, if used, adding enough milk to give the mixture a soft dropping consistency.

Turn the mixture into a well greased small loaf tin, and gently level the surface. Bake in the pre-heated oven for about 30-40 minutes, until the loaf is well risen and firm to the touch. Take out of the oven and allow the loaf to cool in the tin for about 5 minutes, then turn out on to a wire rack.

—·—

Harvest Home

The 'harvest home', when the last of the harvest had been brought in, was traditionally celebrated on the farms of the north-east of England with a harvest supper, known by various names such as 'mell supper', 'cream pot', 'kern supper', or 'churn supper'.

Thropton, Simonside c1960   T227025

Darlington, The Entrance to Northgate 1926   79026

Stottie Bread

A type of bread that is traditional to the north-east is Stottie, which is particularly good when used to make a bacon sandwich. Stottie is made in the same way as other bread, but the dough is only left to rise, or 'prove' once, rather than twice as is usual when making bread. The housewife would make a Stottie on baking day by taking a piece off the main dough after the first rising and then shaping and cooking it immediately, because she needed bread to make her husband's 'bait', or snack, for him to take to work. The Stottie was then baked at the bottom of the oven in the kitchen range, and so is also known as Oven Bottom Bread. Stotties were especially popular with the miners of the north-east, who often took them down the pit as part of their 'bait' filled with cheese or cold meat, and they are also often known as Geordie Stottie Cakes.

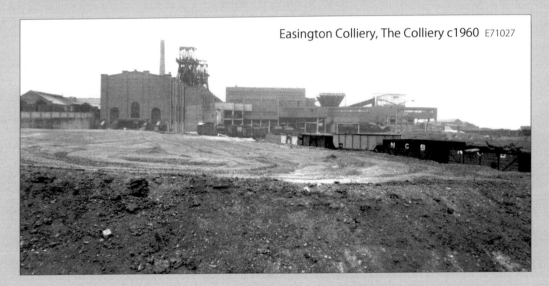

Easington Colliery, The Colliery c1960 E71027

At the time this photograph was taken, Easington was one of six large pits situated along the coast of County Durham; the others were Wearmouth, Vane Tempest, Dawdon Seaham and Horden. Between them they employed over 10,000 men and extracted over 4 million tonnes of coal a year from seams stretching out under the North Sea. Easington closed in 1993.

When the mining industry was nationalised in 1947, there were 127 active pits in County Durham employing 108,000 mineworkers. Output of the combined Durham and Northumberland coalfield in 1951 was 39 million tonnes, with a productivity level of 259 tonnes per man per year.

Thornley, The Colliery 1951 T123008

RECIPE

—·—

Boiled Fruit Cake

This easy to make cake is full of flavour because the dried fruit is cooked in liquid before baking, making it juicy and delicious.

350g/12oz mixed dried fruit - sultanas, raisins and
   currants
115g/4oz caster sugar, or soft brown sugar if preferred
115g/4oz butter or margarine
150ml/ ¼ pint water
1 egg, beaten
225g/8oz self-raising flour

Place the dried fruit, sugar, butter or margarine and water in a large saucepan. Place over a low heat and bring slowly to simmering point. Cover the pan, reduce the heat and simmer gently for 20 minutes, then leave to cool.

Pre-heat the oven to 150°C/300°F/Gas Mark 2.

When the fruit mixture has cooled, stir in the beaten egg. Sieve the flour and stir it into the mixture, which should end up with a dropping consistency, and not be too thick. Turn the mixture into a well-greased 15cm (6 inch) cake tin, and bake in the centre of the pre-heated oven for about 1½ hours, until the top is firm to the touch. Allow to cool in the tin for 5 minutes, then turn out on to a wire tray.

—·—

The Jarrow Crusade

After the collapse of the Jarrow shipbuilding industry in the 1930s the town was left with the highest rate of unemployment in the country, at 70%. In October 1936, 200 men set out from the town to walk 300 miles to London, on a 'hunger march' that has become famous as the Jarrow Crusade. The Crusade was an attempt to get the Government to take notice of the dire straits Jarrow had been left in, and to do something pro-active to attract alternative forms of industry.

The men took 3 weeks and 5 days to reach London, playing mouth organs along the way to keep up their spirits. They slept in schools, drill halls and casualty wards of hospitals along the route; both Labour and Conservative organisations provided baths and hot meals, and relays of medical students cared for blistered feet and other ailments. There was widespread sympathy for the Jarrow Crusade, and the men marched into London in the pouring rain to a huge meeting in Hyde Park.

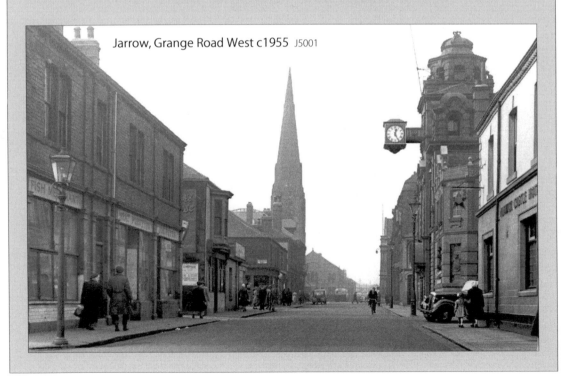

Jarrow, Grange Road West c1955 J5001

Sunderland, Fawcett Street
1890 S263001

RECIPE

—·—

Singin' Hinney

Sit doon, noo, man alive!
Te tell ye aa'll contrive
O' the finest thing the worl' hes iver gin ye, O.
It's not fine claes or drink
Nor owt 'at ye can think
Can had a cannie up ti singin'-hinney, O.

From 'The Singin' Hinney', originally published in the Newcastle Weekly Chronicle in 1885.

This famous girdle (or griddle) cake from the north-east gets its name from the hissing sound that is made during the cooking process, as the cake sizzles and 'sings'. It is a form of fried scone. It should be eaten whilst it is still hot, cut into wedges and spread with butter. Traditionally a Singin' Hinney would be cooked whole and turned with special wooden 'hands' to prevent it breaking. If turning the Hinney proves difficult, try sliding the Hinney from the girdle on to a plate, then turning it over onto another plate and sliding it back on to the girdle. Alternatively, the Hinney can be cut into quarters before cooking.

115g/4oz plain flour
½ teaspoonful baking powder
¼ teaspoonful of salt
25g/1oz butter
25g/1oz lard
25g/1oz caster sugar
25g/1oz currants or sultanas
About 2 tablespoonfuls of milk and/or single or sour cream to mix

Sieve together the flour, baking powder and salt. Rub in the fats until the mixture resembles fine breadcrumbs, then add the sugar and the currants or sultanas. Mix to a soft dough with a little milk and knead it lightly. Form the dough into a ball, then flatten it to make a round of dough about 20cm (8 inches) across and about 1cm (½ inch thick).

Grease a girdle (griddle) or a large heavy frying pan, and place over the heat. Prick the top of the Hinney lightly with a fork, place on the girdle or pan and cook for about 8-10 minutes on each side, turning it once, until it is golden and firm. The griddle should be re-greased between cooking each side.

—·—

Darlington, North Lodge Park 1911 63547

South Shields, Laygate Lane 1900 S162001

INDEX OF PHOTOGRAPHS

INDEX OF RECIPES

Haltwhistle c1900 H344301

NOTES

FRITH PRODUCTS & SERVICES

Francis Frith would doubtless be pleased to know that the pioneering publishing venture he started in 1860 still continues today. Over a hundred and forty years later, The Francis Frith Collection continues in the same innovative tradition and is now one of the foremost publishers of vintage photographs in the world. Some of the current activities include:

INTERIOR DECORATION

Today Frith's photographs can be seen framed and as giant wall murals in thousands of pubs, restaurants, hotels, banks, retail stores and other public buildings throughout the country. In every case they enhance the unique local atmosphere of the places they depict and provide reminders of gentler days in an increasingly busy and frenetic world.

PRODUCT PROMOTIONS

Frith products are used by many major companies to promote the sales of their own products or to reinforce their own history and heritage. Frith promotions have been used by Hovis bread, Courage beers, Scots Porage Oats, Colman's mustard, Cadbury's foods, Mellow Birds coffee, Dunhill pipe tobacco, Guinness, and Bulmer's Cider.

GENEALOGY AND FAMILY HISTORY

As the interest in family history and roots grows world-wide, more and more people are turning to Frith's photographs of Great Britain for images of the towns, villages and streets where their ancestors lived; and, of course, photographs of the churches and chapels where their ancestors were christened, married and buried are an essential part of every genealogy tree and family album.

FRITH PRODUCTS

All Frith photographs are available Framed or just as Mounted Prints and Posters (size 23 x 16 inches). These may be ordered from the address below. Other products available are- Address Books, Calendars, Jigsaws, Canvas Prints, Notelets and local and prestige books.

THE INTERNET

Already ninety thousand Frith photographs can be viewed and purchased on the internet through the Frith websites and a myriad of partner sites.

For more detailed information on Frith companies and products, look at this site:
www.francisfrith.com

See the complete list of Frith Books at: www.francisfrith.com
This web site is regularly updated with the latest list of publications from The Francis Frith Collection. If you wish to buy books relating to another part of the country that your local bookshop does not stock, you may purchase on-line.

For further information, trade, or author enquiries please contact us at the address below:
The Francis Frith Collection, Unit 6, Oakley Business Park, Wylye Road, Dinton, Wiltshire SP3 5EU.
Tel: +44 (0)1722 716 376   Fax: +44 (0)1722 716 881   Email: sales@francisfrith.co.uk

---

See Frith products on the internet at www.francisfrith.com

FREE PRINT OF YOUR CHOICE

Mounted Print
Overall size 14 x 11 inches (355 x 280mm)

Choose any Frith photograph in this book.
Simply complete the Voucher opposite and return it with your remittance for £3.50 (to cover postage and handling) and we will print the photograph of your choice in SEPIA (size 11 x 8 inches) and supply it in a cream mount with a burgundy rule line (overall size 14 x 11 inches).
Please note: aerial photographs and photographs with a reference number starting with a "Z" are not Frith photographs and cannot be supplied under this offer. Offer valid for delivery to one UK address only.

PLUS: Order additional Mounted Prints at HALF PRICE - £9.50 each (normally £19.00)
If you would like to order more Frith prints from this book, possibly as gifts for friends and family, you can buy them at half price (with no additional postage and handling costs).

PLUS: Have your Mounted Prints framed
For an extra £18.00 per print you can have your mounted print(s) framed in an elegant polished wood and gilt moulding, overall size 16 x 13 inches (no additional postage and handling required).

IMPORTANT!

These special prices are only available if you use this form to order. You must use the ORIGINAL VOUCHER on this page (no copies permitted). We can only despatch to one UK address. This offer cannot be combined with any other offer.

Send completed Voucher form to:
The Francis Frith Collection, Unit 6, Oakley Business Park, Wylye Road, Dinton, Wiltshire SP3 5EU

CHOOSE A PHOTOGRAPH FROM THIS BOOK

Voucher for **FREE** and Reduced Price *Frith Prints*

Please do not photocopy this voucher. Only the original is valid, so please fill it in, cut it out and return it to us with your order.

Picture ref no	Page no	Qty	Mounted @ £9.50	Framed + £18.00	Total Cost £
		1	Free of charge*	£	£
			£9.50	£	£
			£9.50	£	£
			£9.50	£	£
			£9.50	£	£
			£9.50	£	£
Please allow 28 days for delivery. Offer available to one UK address only			* Post & handling		£3.50
			Total Order Cost		£

Title of this book . . . .
I enclose a cheque/postal order for £ . . . .
made payable to 'The Francis Frith Collection'

OR please debit my Mastercard / Visa / Maestro card, details below

Card Number:

Issue No (Maestro only):   Valid from (Maestro):

Card Security Number: Expires:

Signature:

Name Mr/Mrs/Ms . . . .
Address . . . .
. . . .
. . . . Postcode . . . .
Daytime Tel No . . . .
Email . . . .

Valid to 31/12/12

Can you help us with information about any of the Frith photographs in this book?

We are gradually compiling an historical record for each of the photographs in the Frith archive. It is always fascinating to find out the names of the people shown in the pictures, as well as insights into the shops, buildings and other features depicted.

If you recognize anyone in the photographs in this book, or if you have information not already included in the author's caption, do let us know. We would love to hear from you, and will try to publish it in future books or articles.

An Invitation from The Francis Frith Collection to Share Your Memories

The 'Share Your Memories' feature of our website allows members of the public to add personal memories relating to the places featured in our photographs, or comment on others already added. Seeing a place from your past can rekindle forgotten or long held memories. Why not visit the website, find photographs of places you know well and add YOUR story for others to read and enjoy? We would love to hear from you!

www.francisfrith.com/memories

Our production team

Frith books are produced by a small dedicated team at offices near Salisbury. Most have worked with the Frith Collection for many years. All have in common one quality: they have a passion for the Frith Collection.

Frith Books and Gifts

We have a wide range of books and gifts available on our website utilising our photographic archive, many of which can be individually personalised.

www.francisfrith.com